Précis Writing for

Guy Noel Pocock

Alpha Editions

This edition published in 2024

ISBN 9789361471902

Design and Setting By

Alpha Editions
www.alphaedis.com

Email - info@alphaedis.com

As per information held with us this book is in Public Domain.
This book is a reproduction of an important historical work.
Alpha Editions uses the best technology to reproduce historical work
in the same manner it was first published to preserve its original nature.
Any marks or number seen are left intentionally to preserve.

Contents

FOREWORD	- 1 -
PRÉCIS WRITING	- 2 -
What Précis Means	- 2 -
The Object of these Exercises	- 2 -
How to tackle a Précis	- 2 -
"Reported Speech"	- 3 -
No. 1.—Exercises in "Reported Speech"	- 5 -
Notes	- 6 -
No. 2.—George Oakes	- 7 -
Notes	- 8 -
No. 3.—The Cobra	- 9 -
Notes	- 10 -
No. 4.—The Two Lieutenants	- 11 -
Notes	- 13 -
No. 5.—The Black Republic	- 14 -
Notes	- 16 -
No. 6.—The Professor and the Monkeys	- 17 -
No. 7.—The Island	- 19 -
Notes	- 21 -
No. 8.—A Seventeenth-Century Witch Trial	- 22 -
Notes	- 24 -
No. 9.—The Miser	- 25 -
Notes	- 27 -
No. 10.—The Boy Scouts	- 28 -
Notes	- 30 -

No. 11.—Child Labourers in 1836	- 31 -
Notes	- 33 -
No. 12.—The Museum, 300 B.C.	- 34 -
Notes	- 36 -
No. 13.—The Warning	- 37 -
Notes	- 40 -
No. 14.—Science as taught in our Great-grandfathers' School-days	- 41 -
Notes	- 44 -
No. 15—The Hut-Tax	- 45 -
Notes	- 49 -
No. 16.—The Mandarin	- 50 -
Notes	- 54 -
No. 17—Isaac Newton	- 55 -
Notes	- 57 -
No. 18.—The Battle of the Nile	- 58 -

FOREWORD

The object of this little book is to teach précis writing from the very start. It has been found from experience that the average boy who in the Lower Fifth Form starts making précis of Government Blue Books and Collected Correspondence, will flounder about for a whole term without understanding what he is really expected to do.

The following exercises are progressive and the rules of strict précis writing are learnt one by one. The exercises are really very simple parodies of Government Reports, &c., such as a boy will have to deal with in the higher forms and the Army Examinations. They are arranged in groups, e.g. *Reports, Correspondence, Trials, Ships' Logs,* and so forth. After working through the series a boy should be perfectly competent to tackle the real thing.

Incidentally, there is no better training than précis writing for concentration of thought and expression.

G. N. P.

ROYAL NAVAL COLLEGE, DARTMOUTH.
April, 1917.

PRÉCIS WRITING

What Précis Means

A précis is the essence of a longer story of any kind. You take your story and 'boil it down', so as to get rid of all the parts that do not really matter; you then collect what is left, and put these points together in a short concise 'summary'. But the result must not be a 'list' of important points, or a series of 'jottings'. It must be the same story told clearly and readably, in a very much condensed form.

For instance, you may have to make a précis of a long pile of letters dealing with some particular subject; or perhaps the account of a trial; or a long report written by one individual. It doesn't matter what the longer 'story' is. What you have to do is to read it through, extract all the parts that matter, and put them down in readable form.

The Object of these Exercises

Now précis writing is unlike free English composition. It is much more exact and scientific; and it must be written according to certain definite rules. It is no use trying to learn all the rules at once; you will learn them one by one, and without trouble, as you work through the following exercises.

These exercises are not the *real* Government Blue Books, reports, trials, &c., that you will have to tackle later on. They are all 'made up'. But they are exactly like the real thing. The only difference is that they are much easier and shorter—and they are not so dull. And as they are the same sort of thing on a small scale, you should be able to deal with the real ones later on when you meet them.

How to tackle a Précis

All précis, whether easy or difficult, should be tackled in the same way. First read the whole thing through very carefully without writing any notes or underlining any passages.

All depends on this first reading. For if you once get into the way of writing your précis or even making notes 'as you go along', you will never grasp the subject as a whole. And the result will be that your précis will lack balance. Either you will write too much about the first half and skimp the rest, or you will write a great deal about the picturesque points that appeal to you, and leave out things that really matter.

When you have read it carefully through, and got the whole story in your mind, run through it quickly a second time marking the passages you mean to use. For the purposes of this book the best plan will be to underline in pencil those passages which will have to be used with little alteration, and to put a wavy line against those which cannot be left out altogether, but must be greatly condensed.

Last, work up all the marked passages into a short continuous 'story'.

RULE I.—**Start your Précis with a title.**

This title must not be of the imaginative kind that would suit a story, such as 'A Misunderstanding', or 'The Adventures of a Red Cross Man'. It must be a clear and concise statement of what the précis is about. Thus: "Précis of the correspondence between the British Government and Dr. Wilson, President of the United States, concerning contraband of war". And if dates are given you should add, "between Feb. 18, 1915, and Oct., 1916".

RULE II.—**Every Précis must be written in the form of REPORTED SPEECH.**

This rule is so important that it is impossible to write a précis till it is thoroughly understood. It will be necessary to explain what is meant by 'reported speech', and to practise a few examples.

"Reported Speech"

Suppose you say to somebody, "I can't be bothered, as I am busy writing a précis!" you are using a form which is called Direct speech. And suppose the person you were addressing goes away and says to somebody else, "So-and-so said he couldn't be bothered, as he was busy writing a précis", he is *reporting* what you said. In other words, he has turned your 'direct speech' into 'reported speech'.

Notice what has happened. You are no longer the person speaking, but the person spoken about: therefore 'I' becomes 'he'. Also you are no longer speaking: what you said is now 'in the past'; therefore 'can't' becomes 'could not' and 'am' becomes 'was'.

This is quite straightforward. The difficulty arises when you are dealing with words that imply future time. Without going into the syntax, one may just explain that in Reported speech the 'future' must be referred back to the time at which the Direct statement was spoken. Thus: "I will write when I get home", becomes "He said that he *would* write when he *got* home".

Thus for the purposes of simple précis writing the following rules must be observed:—

(*a*) Never use the First or Second persons: always the Third.

(*b*) Never use the Present tense: always the Past.

(*c*) Never use the Future tense: always refer it back to the past. Even a verb such as 'must', which usually implies the future, should be changed to 'would have to', or some such phrase.

(*d*) Possessive adjectives, my, your, our, must be changed to the Third person.

(*e*) Adverbs and adverbial phrases must be changed in the same way. 'Now' becomes 'then'; 'at the present time' becomes 'at that time'; 'here' becomes 'there', and so on.

Take one more example. You know this familiar quotation: "I will arise and go to my Father, and say unto Him, 'Father, I have sinned against Heaven and before Thee, and am no more worthy to be called Thy son'".

Now suppose you were telling the story of the Prodigal Son to a Japanese gentleman, or somebody who had not heard it before, and you wished to keep pretty close to the original, you might put it in this way: "The prodigal son then determined that he would arise and go to his Father, and confess that he had sinned before Him and against Heaven, and was no more worthy to be called His son".

Compare these two forms, and note all the differences.

No. 1.—Exercises in "Reported Speech"

(1.) The following are written in the form of Direct speech. Rewrite them in Reported speech:—

(*a*) "Sister Anne, sister Anne, do you see anyone coming?" asked the poor wife again.

"I see nothing but a cloud of dust," her sister replied.

(*b*) "I cannot speak to you here and now; but after the match is over I shall take the first opportunity of telling you exactly what I think of you."

(*c*) "I don't know whether I shall be able to come. I will if I can, but that must depend on how things turn out. At this moment I cannot say definitely that I will come."

(2.) Report the following speech, beginning thus:—

"On rising to introduce Mr. Elijah Timmins, the mayor elect, the retiring mayor said that...."

"Gentlemen, I have the honour to bring to your notice Mr. Elijah Timmins, who is to be your mayor for the coming year. Mr. Timmins, gentlemen, has had—not the experience *I* have had, of course, for *my* experience has been exceptional. I have had a hard struggle, gentlemen, but by solid work and honest dealing—and you will bear me out when I say that my pork sausages are always of the highest order—I raised myself to the top of the tree. Modesty forbids me to speak of myself, gentlemen; but I have felt that in these times of war and stress it is very important to have at the helm a mayor of real tact and business capacity; and I cannot help thinking that I have been the right man in the right place. With Lord Nelson I may say, 'Thank God I have done my duty'.

"Mr. Timmins, gentlemen, is about to step into my shoes; and I only trust he will not undo the good work that I have done."

We are now in a position to write précis in its simplest form. We will try a few very easy examples first, such as "George Oakes" and the "Cobra"; after that the exercises will become more difficult.

Notes

The following is a letter written by an old cottager to the Squire of his Parish. Condense it to half the length, correcting the spelling and grammar. It is very simple, as there is only one 'subject', and therefore only one paragraph. But it will serve to introduce this most important rule of Précis writing:

RULE III.—**All points essential to the subject MUST be put in; while all unessential points, repetitions, &c., should be left out.**

(We may modify the second half of this rule later on.)

Remember that it must be written as 'reported speech'.

No. 2.—George Oakes

Ivy Cottage,
Bourton-on-the-Water.

Dear Sir,

I ope you are quite well as this leaves me at present which my wife as the swolen glans something bitter but I do not complain it being the Will of God, which my wife do so most monotinous. Dear Sir I ave been out of work Severn weeks come Toosdy and the price of coals is rose something crool which I cannot afford them nohow, and my wife havin the swolen glans and wot not. Dear Sir if you could give me a job of work in the garden or the fowlouse I should take it most grateful bein bread and born in the fowlouse in a manner of speakin sixty years man and boy I ave ad truck with fowls. Dear Sir you ave the oner to know me so long there is no need of Referances, which perraps you might not ave heard my experance in the foulouse which believe me sir I understands all manner of Fowls, poultry and wot not, and my wife as ad truck with ducks but she bein laid aside with the swolen glans she cannot come out which bein the Will of God I do not complain. Dear Sir perraps you would like to give me a trial seein as how I do not live far a way bein strong in the Legs. Dear Sir if you will give me a Trial I will take it most kind.

Dear Sir God bless you and trousers you give me are fine and warm as everso which they are a bit narrer but not to mention.

Yours umble Dear Sir

George Oakes.

Notes

The following is also very simple, and may be done in one paragraph of ten or twelve lines.

Make up your mind what the real subject of this paragraph should be; and notice that the colonel is not really of the slightest importance to the story—except that he tells it.

Don't forget the title, beginning "Précis of …".

No. 3.—The Cobra

"Talking of snakes," said the colonel, pushing back his chair and lighting another cheroot, "reminds me of a curious incident that happened when I was stationed at Ghurrapore, in the early 'eighties. Ghurrapore was an infernal bad place for snakes, and the worst of the lot was the cobra or hooded snake. These cobras, or hooded snakes, turned up everywhere—in your bath, under the verandah, anywhere. Now, one day one of my officers, Lieutenant Simpson, went into the officers' changing-room to get a pair of tennis shoes. There were a dozen pairs in a wooden box; and not seeing his own on the top he put his hand in to fish out the bottom ones. Now you must know that there had been a regular plague of cobras, or hooded snakes, in the lines, and we were all a bit panicky; so when Simpson suddenly felt something pricking him, and drew out his hand to find two drops of blood on his little finger, he at once concluded it was a cobra, or hooded snake.

"I was sitting in the club at the time drinking some of that excellent 7 star whisky—you remember it, Major? And when I saw young Simpson running across the compound holding his little finger, I at once said to myself, 'That's a hooded snake or cobra!'

"I then followed him to the carpenter's shop; but by the time I got there the thing was done. He had taken a heavy chisel, and cut his little finger right off! I helped him back to the club, sent for the doctor, and gave Simpson a dose of that 7 star whisky—you remember it, Major? I then sent four men to the changing-room armed with sticks. We upset the box and beat those shoes unmercifully—but no cobra or hooded snake! When I felt that the situation was quite safe, I myself examined the box. And there sticking up through the bottom boards were two little nails, sharp and close together! And so young Simpson had cut his finger off for nothing! Infernal bad luck I call it. Infernal bad luck. For anyone—even I myself—would easily have mistaken the 'bite' for that of a cobra, or hooded snake."

Notes

The following is a study in contrasts. The rest is really quite subsidiary. Bring out this point by means of contrasting paragraphs.

Condense the descriptions of the characters as much as you can, without leaving out more points than you can help.

No. 4.—The Two Lieutenants

Extract from the Autobiography of Admiral Sir Hercules Prout, K.C.B.

"... The sphere of influence of the British Navy comprising as it does the waters of the entire globe, it follows that the average naval officer comes into contact with all sorts and conditions of men; and if he uses his opportunities he will inevitably become a rare judge of human character. He will tend to range men in groups whether they be his own officers or men, or persons of every race and grade of society with whom he comes into contact.

"Captains of H.M. Ships are often called upon to use powers of selection and discrimination. I recall one particular instance in which I was called upon to select from among my junior officers one who could carry through a difficult and dangerous business, the success or failure of which would be attended with far-reaching consequences. No matter now what the business was. Suffice to say that it was connected with gun-running on the part of certain unfriendly chiefs, and indirectly with the influence of a so-called friendly European power. A delicate business requiring rare qualities of daring and tact, and an aptitude for diplomacy and espionage.

"I retired to my cabin and went through the list of all officers above the rank of midshipman, crossing out the unsuitable till I had reduced my choice to two. These I will call Lieutenant X and Lieutenant Z.

"Lieutenant X was a very large and powerful fellow, with fair hair and blue-grey eyes—a typical Saxon. He was a magnificent athlete and had played back for the Navy. He was a clever fellow too—I had noticed that—though he pretended not to be. His manner was boisterous and frank, and sometimes he used this as bluff. (I recall several instances—but that is neither here nor there.) He was very popular, for he 'had a way with him', and often made people tell him things when they had had no intention of doing so. His manner was so pleasant that most people failed to realize how masterful he was. As a boy on the *Britannia* he had been a strong chief cadet captain, and yet contrived to be very popular. Add to this he was a capital seaman, and could turn his hand to anything, especially in emergency; and in those days and that part of the world emergencies were frequent.

"Lieutenant Z was the very antithesis of Lieutenant X both in appearance and manner. He was small and dark and wiry; his features were very clean-cut, and his thin lips pressed tightly together in a perfectly straight line gave an impression of immense determination. He was then quite one of the cleverest lieutenants in the Navy, and as shrewd as he was clever. He was very reticent, and he possessed a 'biting' tongue, if one may be allowed a queer metaphor; no one ever knew what he was thinking about unless he told them, and then he often told them what he did not really think. And so he was feared but not liked. I had never known him to be taken by surprise; and he was an absolutely dead shot with a revolver.

"After taking into consideration all the possible circumstances with which my emissary was likely to be faced, I made my decision, and sent for Lieutenant Z. I need hardly say that I had every ground for satisfaction with my choice; but Z's adventures must be told in another chapter."

Notes

The following exercise is again a study in contrasts, but in this case there are *more than two*.

You will have seen from the last exercise that the way to make your précis clear is to arrange all the topics in separate paragraphs.

We may put it in the form of a Rule:

RULE IV.—**After you have stated your main subject in the 'title', arrange all the different topics in SEPARATE PARAGRAPHS; and whenever you can, make the 'state of affairs' clear in your first paragraph.**

This rule applies to every précis you write. The best plan is to jot down in pencil Headings for all your paragraphs before you start writing your précis (three in short précis; four, five, or six, in longer précis). The length of each paragraph depends on the importance of the topic.

No. 5.—The Black Republic

Extract from the reminiscences of Commander Brown, R.N.

I have only once visited the Black Republic, and that was some years ago, when I was still a midshipman. I was in the *Argo* then, a curious old tub that has long since been scrapped. We had been cruising about the islands and enjoying ourselves hugely, when the captain received orders to bring certain pressure to bear upon the Black Republicans. I don't know what the fuss was about; that didn't concern me. What did interest me was the fact that we—myself and four other "snotties"—were allowed shore-leave for the afternoon.

A strange wild place the island looked as we approached it in the picket-boat: a huge tumbled mass of bare mountain peaks, for all the world like a crumpled newspaper thrown down on a blue carpet. It was beautiful too in this glare of the tropical sun, with its gleaming grey rocks and dark forest belt, and the straggling lines of white houses that backed the harbour.

As we drew nearer we could see the yellow lateen sails of little fruit-boats that crowded round the quay, the green sun-blinds of houses, and the white dresses and brilliant red and blue parasols of the ladies who thronged the promenade—a regular kaleidoscope of dazzling colour points. And we promised ourselves a jolly afternoon of exploration and ramble.

But no sooner had we rounded the mole and entered the harbour than the whole aspect changed. It is difficult to convey a true impression of the extreme shabbiness and tawdriness of the scene. It fell like a blight upon us, and our spirits sank down into our boots. The whole surface of the harbour was covered with a scum of dirt and oil in which floated banana skins, bits of orange-peel, matches, and dead flies, while the quay was pervaded by an indescribable stench, heavy and sweet, like an old dust-bin.

We came alongside and walked up the steps, slipping on fishes' heads and fruit skins; and everywhere we were met by the same dirty finery and pretentious tawdriness. Crowds of ladies walked up and down the parade—black ladies, dressed in dirty white frocks and darned canvas shoes. Their brilliant parasols were torn, and their hat-feathers dishevelled like those of a scare-crow.

Innumerable soldiers—black men, of course—thronged the streets, strutting with indescribable self-satisfaction. But they were as shabby as the "ladies", in their dirty cocked-hats, their concertina-like trousers, and tunics stuck all over with medals and orders like Christmas-trees. We discovered from the Commander afterwards that the whole army consists of officers, very few of them below the rank of Major-general. They are inordinately proud of their medals, and quite amazingly inefficient.

It was really beastly—there is no other word to describe it—so beastly that we snotties walked along in silence, unable at first to realize how funny it all was. Presently a huge black major-general, decked with gold tinsel epaulets and as many orders as the Lord High Executioner, came across to us and saluted with magnificent gusto.

"What the deuce does the old buffer want?" whispered Jones to me.

"Me speak Englees," said the major-general, and paused.

"Well, out with it, old son; what do you want?" asked Jones disrespectfully.

And then at last we saw the humour of the whole ramshackle system; for what in the world should this affected old turkey-cock of a major-general want, but to carry the bag which contained our towels and tea for the modest sum of half a crown! We roared with laughter; and at that moment our 1st Lieutenant came along.

"Get out! no want!" he said; and the disconcerted major-general slunk away with the most humorous expression of offended pride and grovelling servility.

"I shouldn't stay in the town," said the lieutenant; "it stinks. If you carry on down the road, you will come to a first-rate bathing-place."

And so we did.

Notes

A short paragraph of explanation is needed. The different lines of investigation fit very easily into different paragraphs.

No. 6.—The Professor and the Monkeys

Translation of a letter written by Herr Professor Otto von Pumpenstein to the München Philological Society.

WILHELMSTRASSE, HAMBURG.
June 1.

GENTLEMEN,

I regret that distance prohibits me from attending the summer meeting of the Philological Society in person; more especially as I have been making certain investigations which, I venture to think, will have far-reaching consequences. Allow me to enclose the report of my experiments.

ihr ergebenst

OTTO VON PUMPENSTEIN.

Enclosure

Report of certain experiments carried out in the Monkey-house of the Hamburg Zoological Gardens.

The following experiments were made by me by kind permission of the Herr Vorsteher of the Zoological Gardens, with the object of ascertaining whether monkeys actually converse in language. I was drawn to make these experiments by a consideration of the extraordinary similarity between the structure of the mouth and vocal chords in Man and the Anthropoid Apes, and by the amazing correspondence between their brain-charts. I accordingly had a small travelling cage fitted up with table, ink-stand, and so forth, and placed inside the large cage of the chimpanzees, which happened to be next that of the spider monkeys, in such a position that I could enter it without fear of attack.

In this cage I spent my holiday, arriving at the Monkey-house at 10 every morning, and leaving at 6 p.m. My meals I took when the chimpanzees were fed, to avoid arousing jealousy. During the first week I filled five notebooks with the noises made by these animals (spelt phonetically), but without being able to attach any particular thought to any of them. My first success was the result of flashing a mirror in the eyes of the old male chimpanzee. He invariably showed signs of distress, beat the wires of my cage, and said, "Kee—kee—r-r-r-t!" which would seem to mean, "This I can no longer stand!" I tried this experiment on 105 occasions, and always with the same result.

My next success was with regard to the spider monkeys. I discovered that by singing a particular note I could induce these monkeys to imitate me in a very shrill strident tone, but always in perfect pitch. In a few days' time they could sing up and down the scale, but without any articulation. I next sang them "Deutschland, Deutschland über alles" in a loud voice. They received the first few lines in silence, and were then seized with a wild enthusiasm, gathering handfuls of bran and flinging them into my cage. Since that experiment I have so far been unable to induce them to sing.

I next carried out a series of important experiments with the aid of a gramophone. Observing that an old fierce chimpanzee was kept in a cage by himself, I induced his keeper to deprive him of water for several hours. I then approached a basin of water to the outside of the beast's cage, placing the gramophone close to his mouth as he hung by one foot from the ceiling. I took a record of his remarks, which appeared to consist of a repetition of the word "G-r-r-ump". I then carried the record to my original cage and turned it on. My first trials were unsuccessful, but on the fifteenth repetition I observed that an old female chimpanzee pushed her saucer of water in my direction. From this I concluded that the meaning of the old ape's remark was, "I a drink of water want". I have made a great number of experiments with the gramophone, and am inclined to believe that the chimpanzee for "nut" is "warra-yak"; "banana" is "kee-e" (very shrill), and so forth.

I shall spend another fortnight in my cage, and I confidently hope for still more startling and far-reaching results. I have attempted to reproduce these noises, or phrases, myself; but so far they have not been received in a friendly spirit.

No. 7.—The Island

Report of Captain H. Cardew, R.N., on the condition of the Island of Ingelos.

H.M.S. *Dundonald*, off St. Helena.
June 1.

To the Colonial Secretary.

SIR,

I have the honour to inform you that I have just returned from a visit to the island of Ingelos, and I herewith submit my report.

The *Dundonald* was the first ship to visit this island since October, 1910, though an Italian brigantine was wrecked there a year ago. (All the crew were drowned with the exception of the cook, one Antonio Posillippo, who has since married and settled down, and has no intention of leaving.)

The inhabitants consist of 38 men, 30 women, and 23 children. Their Head-man is John Brown, grandson of the original John Brown who was wrecked there in 1848. They appear to be happy and contented, and there has never been any illness on the island, barring a virulent cold in the head started by Posillippo a few days after his rescue. The original flock of goats does exceedingly well on the mountain, providing the community with milk, cheese, and goats' flesh; while the islanders have developed a wonderful capacity for fishing under difficult conditions. Potatoes do very well, and the yearly wheat crop is most carefully looked after.

The Head-man told me that the community had suffered very seriously for many months from a plague of rats, the ancestors of which had swum ashore from the wrecked brigantine. They swarm in prodigious numbers, spoiling crops and even killing kids. The ship's terrier wrought great havoc during our three days' stay, and I have left several tins of rat-poison. Under the direction of the ship's carpenter some 50 rat-traps were constructed, and the people are setting to work to make many more.

The Head-man is deeply religious and possesses the Bible that belonged to the original John Brown. He conducts a service on the day after every new moon—for there are no "days of the week". We attended one of these services, and found it to consist of a strange mixture of traditions, very crude, but reverent. The Chaplain has given the Head-man a prayer-book.

All the inhabitants talk and read English, but their language is interspersed with a large number of Italian and Spanish words imported by wrecked mariners. There are a certain number of words that appear to be indigenous, such as "skat" and "glob"—the names of certain fish; "latté" for porridge, and "lootoos" for the long goat-skin waders that the fishers wear to protect their legs from stinging fish.

The island is quite self-supporting; but the Head-man is anxious to have a telescope, and knives of all sorts would be exceedingly useful. The people are very grateful for the illuminated texts and pocket-handkerchiefs sent out in the *Dundonald*, and they are wearing both upon their persons.

The education of the children is entirely in the hands of the Head-man Brown.

I have the honour to be,

Your obt. Servt.

H. CARDEW,
Captain R.N.

Notes

The following three exercises are short accounts of trials and investigations.

RULE V.—**In making a précis of the evidence of various witnesses DO NOT PROCEED BY QUESTION AND ANSWER. It is often convenient to keep the evidence of different witnesses in separate paragraphs, but do not repeat the same points. Just tell the story in your own words, and as far as possible in the order in which events happened.**

In making a précis of the Witch Trial be careful to write in modern English.

No. 8.—A Seventeenth-Century Witch Trial

The fourteenth day of the third month in the year of Grace 1616, His most gracious, learned, and religious Majesty King James I being on throne, was brought to trial at Quarter Sessions one Mistress Banbury, charged with having correspondence with the Prince of Darkness, and of practising the detestable rites of witchcraft, whereby sundry persons suffered grievous harm. Whereof the evidence of witnesses was thus and thus.

Master Mark Rubbleyard duly sworn. May it please your worship, on Wednesday last at high noon I and my servants, having felled certain trees in Bishop's copse, and having tied them upon a wain, did drive by the cottage of Mistress Banbury. Now the trees being large and the branches thereof stretching athwartwise, they catched upon the fence of Mistress Banbury's garden. And thereupon, incontinent looked forth Mistress Banbury, and in a loud voice put a curse upon me, upon my horses, and upon my wain. And the curse was of such power that the wain did fall into the ditch ere reaching my farm; moreover, my horses are fallen sick and eat not their oats, and I myself am stricken with a grievous colic.

Mistress Kate Brokedish duly sworn. May it please your worship. Not long since came Mistress Banbury to my house selling simples and charms. And may it please your worship, I did purchase certain snails stewed in milk as a cure for my goodman's warts. And as I made my purchase she did maliciously cast her eyes upon my son Nicholas, he being two years old. And before the day was out my son Nicholas was smitten with a cough and did spit pins until the evening.

Master Noak, Beadle, duly sworn. May it please your worship. Yesternight three lads of the village passing by the house of Mistress Banbury, she cast an evil eye upon them; and they being affrighted threw sundry stones. Whereupon did Mistress Banbury curse them roundly, debeasting herself with detestable oaths. And incontinent the lads have become crossed-eyed, and do hourly vomit forth needles.

Questioned as to whether she were in league with the Devil, Mistress Banbury answered, Yea; howsoever, not with the Prince of Darkness, but with three demons. On being questioned as to their names, she replied, "Pluck, Catch, and Chitabob." On being questioned as to which had forced her to do these things, she replied, "Chitabob did this thing." Then said the judge unto her that was accused: Mistress Banbury, you are accused of the most heinous crime of witchcraft before God and man. Whereof to make an ensample, and to insure right judgement, I hereby give order that your thumbs and your great toes be tied together as it were in the form of a cross, and that you be cast into Tiddler's Pond. And if the sacred element receive you, and mercifully you shall be drowned, then is your innocence approved. But if the sacred element cast you upon its surface and you swim, then is your guilt proven; your body shall be burnt unto death, and your soul shall enter into torment.

Notes

The following exercise will obviously work out at five paragraphs:—In the first tell the 'state of affairs'; in the others give the evidence of the various witnesses without repeating or overlapping more than is necessary.

Remember that the story must be told in good English, not in the language of the witnesses.

No. 9.—The Miser

Evidence concerning the death of Mr. Timothy Keek, of No. 215A Tapley Street, Bristol; before Mr. Jules Curtis.

Evidence of 1st witness in answer to questions.

My name is Clara Cloggs. I am a charwoman and charred for Mr. Keek regular. Once a fortnight, Fridays, I done his room out with soap and soda and opened the winders and made the bed. No, he never had no fires. I was charring on the 3rd floor at 11 o'clock Friday, leaving Mr. Keek's room to the last, as per usual. I knocks at his door with the broom-'andle, which there was no answer. Mrs. 'Uggins from 2nd floor calls up, "He ain't been down for his walk yet, Mrs. Cloggs!" I tries the door, which it were no good; so I calls to Mrs. 'Uggins, "Mrs. 'Uggins!" I sez, "we better fetch the perlice," I sez; "and I for one don't want to be mixed up with no locked doors and suchlike!" I sez. So me and Mrs. 'Uggins fetched the perlice sergeant; and me, I goes 'ome to mind the children's dinner.

Evidence of 2nd witness.

I am Police Constable Blades, 7X. On Friday, 11.20 a.m. precise, I was on my beat between Tapley Street and the King's Arms, when I was met by Mrs. Cloggs and Mrs. 'Uggins, which they are both well known to me. They told me of the business in 'and, and me and Mrs. 'Uggins proceeds to the apartment of Mr. Keek, which we reached it at 11.32 a.m. I then knocked smartly on the door with the knuckles of the left 'and. Receiving no reply I continued the process, at the same time sending Mrs. 'Uggins for the poker. I then broke open the door, and discovered the deceased Mr. Keek at the table with his 'ead on his arms, and his arms on a pile of golden sovereigns. Two or three thousand at a rough estimate. I then whistled for assistance, and sent Mrs. 'Uggins for the doctor. This was at 11.53 a.m. precise.

Evidence of 3rd witness.

Mrs. Jane 'Uggins I am. Yes I knew Mr. Keek, five years I knew 'im. Very quiet regular old gentleman he was. Went out the same time every day, and took his meals out. Couldn't say what his business was—nobody didn't know. I went with Mrs. Cloggs to fetch the perlice. I 'elped Sergeant Blades open Mr. Keek's door, and I see him lying on the sovereigns.

Evidence of 4th witness.

I am Doctor Theodore Simpson. I was fetched to No. 215A Tapley Street at noon on Friday. I found the police in possession of Mr. Keek's room, and Mr. Keek lying across a great pile of gold, as the sergeant told in his evidence. Upon making an examination I found that the deceased had literally died of starvation. He must have been starving himself more or less for years; and for the last few days I should say he had eaten nothing at all.

Notes

Remember that you must not proceed by question and answer. Just tell the story shortly in the order in which events took place.

You will see that it is of no importance whatever to know the *names* of the persons concerned. (If mentioned, they should be enclosed in brackets.) But perhaps it is important to know the *ages* of the boys, as this affects the story.

No. 10.—The Boy Scouts

Part of the evidence taken in the Police Court, in the trial of two boys, Albert Home (16) and James Hopkins (16).

Mr. Carter, J.P. "Your name?"

1st Witness—*a boy scout.* "Tom Appleby, sir."

Mr. C. "Age?"

1st W. "Fourteen-a-half, sir."

Mr. C. "Tell the Court exactly what you were doing on Thursday afternoon."

1st W. "Me and my patrol were doing Spider and Fly—that's a scout game, sir—down below Barley's Farm, and I was creeping through the trees so as not to make no noise when I heard somebody laugh, and when I crawls nearer I sees the—the prisoners sitting on the bank of Barley's duck pond."

Mr. C. "Could you see exactly what they were doing?"

1st W. "Yes, sir. The short one had hold of a frog by the back legs, and the tall one had a bicycle pump, and he put the connection down the frog's throat, and was blowin' him up with the bicycle pump."

Mr. C. "Are you quite certain of this?"

1st W. "Yes, sir; and here's the body all busted." (Frog's body produced.)

Mr. C. "And then what did you do?"

1st W. "Crawled back through the wood and signalled instructions to my patrol, sir. And when we got back they was starting in on another frog."

Mr. C. "And how did you manage to catch these boys? They seem to be much bigger and stronger than any of you."

1st W. "We lassooed 'em with ropes, sir, and pulled 'em backwards, sir, and then all ten of us set on 'em, sir, and tied 'em up, sir!" (Laughter.)

Mr. C. "And how did you get them to the camp?"

1st W. "Semaphored for the 'and-cart, sir." (Laughter.)

2nd Witness called.

Mr. C. "Your name?"

2nd W. "My name is George Collinson."

Mr. C. "You are scoutmaster in charge of the scouts' summer camp, I believe?"

2nd W. "That is so."

Mr. C. "Kindly tell the Court what you saw in connection with this business."

2nd W. "At 3.30 on Thursday afternoon I was returning from the railway station with a newly arrived patrol when I saw a party of scouts coming from the direction of Barley's Farm. They were pulling the small hand-cart in which two boys appeared to be lying. Fearing an accident I ran to meet them, and found these two lads tied securely hand and foot and fastened into the cart by means of the luggage-straps."

Mr. C. "And what orders did you give?"

2nd W. "After hearing the whole story from Tom Appleby, I gave directions that the two lads should be taken to my tent. I also sent into Crickley for the police."

Several scouts were then heard as witnesses; and the two lads, having admitted their cruelty, were sentenced to receive six strokes each with the cane.

Notes

Remember that the evidence concerning the treatment of children is the subject of the following letter. The personal feelings of the clergyman are of secondary importance.

RULE VI.—**Proper Names and Titles must be mentioned when it increases the value of the evidence, or report, or whatever it is, to know WHO IS WRITING OR SPEAKING AND WHOM HE IS ADDRESSING. Otherwise do as you like.**

In the following précis it is obviously important to know both.

No. 11.—Child Labourers in 1836

To the Rt. Rev. the Lord Bishop of Lancaster.

THE VICARAGE,
Aug. 10, 1836.

MY LORD,

Having the welfare of my crowded and poverty-stricken parish at heart, and being very greatly exercised in my mind as to the condition of the children living therein, I have thought it well to write to you giving you a brief outline of certain investigations I have made—of which I am now preparing full reports—in the hope that you will interest yourself in the matter, and bring the question of child labour before the Upper House.

My Lord, to say that I am appalled is to use a euphemism. I am shocked beyond all power of expression. Few of the horrors recounted of the African Slave-trade—now so happily abolished—can surpass the callous cruelties inflicted upon children of our own race, living in our own towns—not only by their task-masters and slave-drivers (for one can use no other term), but by their parents even, who, though not altogether dead to feelings of affection, are so ignorant and so harassed that they cannot grasp the idea that any better system is possible.

Let me cite two or three cases, my Lord, in general terms. (Detailed evidence I reserve for my report.)

First there are the boy chimney-sweepers. Orphan boys of eight, nine, and ten, are given away or even sold by the town authorities—who are only too thankful to be rid of the encumbrance—to abandoned ruffians, who, quite dead to all feelings of pity, treat them worse than they treat their half-starved asses. The boys are flogged incessantly, kicked, and starved; they spend their lives climbing about the chimneys of the district in an atmosphere of soot and filth; and if the work is not done soon enough to suit the slave-drivers, as often as not a fire is lit below, and the boy falls burnt and struggling, half-suffocated with the smoke. And the only excuse that the town authorities bring forward for their connivance at this horrible cruelty, is the fact that "many chimneys in the district are built in the old style, and it is absurd to allow these new-fangled ideas of humanity to interfere with the comfort of the home."

My parish, as you are aware, my Lord, is in the mining area; and I have found by personal investigations that the condition of the children in the pits is worse even than that of the chimney boys. For a miserable wage of one shilling a week, and an occasional extra penny for several hours' work overtime, hundreds of little boys are kept working down in the pits for from twelve to sixteen hours a day. Often the children are so young—very many of them are not more than six or seven years old—and so feeble that they are carried to the pit's mouth by their fathers, and this at four o'clock in the morning. They are then taken down to work all day, even during "meals", and only return to the surface after daylight is over.

I myself have been down the shafts many times, and the sights I have seen there are pitiful in the extreme. The galleries in deep mines are provided with doors and traps, "to prevent inflammable drafts", and children of six are trained to sit by themselves all day long, in the dark, opening and shutting these doors as the trucks pass and repass. Can it be wondered at that these infants often become feeble-minded?

But the lot of the older children is even worse. Little boys of eight and nine are harnessed by chains round the hips to small flat trucks, and these they pull on hands and knees through passages only a couple or two and a half feet high. The mines are very wet, and often these narrow pipes through which the children drag their loads are more than half full of water.

Their food is wretchedly inadequate; they are beaten incessantly to keep them awake, for, as the men have often told me, the boys "will fall asleep over their work"; and their home life, such as it is, is wretched and demoralizing beyond words.

In this letter, my Lord, I can do no more than touch upon the surface of things. But for the sake of countless children's lives, I beg you will interest yourself in this matter, that you will read the full report which I have prepared, and use your great influence towards causing these horrors to cease.

Believe me, my Lord,

Your humble and obedient servant,

H. STOKES.

Notes

In this précis the curator and the Nizam should occupy a very small place. The Museum is the real subject—not the curator.

Arrange the points of interest, and group them in separate paragraphs.

Remember that Euclid was the best-known figure the Museum produced; and treat him accordingly.

No. 12.—The Museum, 300 B.C.

(The Nizam Ramayana Gosh, from the Ganges Valley, is shown over the Museum at Alexandria by the chief Curator.)

If the great Nizam will deign to step through the portico, I will conduct his Mightiness at once to the two great libraries.

Here beneath these two great domes is gathered all the literature and learning of the world. These shelves that you see are loaded with books in papyrus or parchment by the hundred thousand, many of them dispatched from Babylon by the great Alexander himself. This door upon our right leads to the amphitheatre where sages and philosophers debate, while upon our left is the hall of banquets.

As your Mightiness will observe—permit me to throw open the door—it is the hour of the afternoon meal. Here you can see some two thousand students reclining at the feast. (Slave! wine for his Mightiness the Nizam!) We cultivate the luxury of our tables and the subtlety of our cooking to the fullest extent. The dignity and splendour of our dinners is beyond belief. I myself spend many hours a day in quiet mastication and enjoyment.

This door opens straight upon the Porch or Colonnade where the Walking philosophers discuss the Cosmos and digest their dinner. These gardens beyond are set apart for the study of botany. Every species of plant and tree has been collected, from the Pillars of Hercules to the shores of the Euxine, from Mesopotamia to the lands of the Ganges, which your Mightiness honours by his gracious rule.

We have now reached the Zoological Gardens. (The collection of these animals was begun by the great philosopher Aristotle.) Here are wolves from the Northern Isles far beyond the Pillars of Hercules; there are monkeys from Northern Africa; tigers from India; river-horses from the far south; and this—I marvel not that your Mightiness is astonished; but have no fear, they harm neither man nor beast!—here is the camelopard, tallest known of beasts. The neck of this specimen measures seven cubits! Those are the bird-houses, and these are ponds and tanks containing all manner of fish. And here are innumerable pheasants, bred for the philosophers' table.

We now reach the lecture-theatre, and I must lower my voice, for lectures are now in progress. Observe, your Mightiness, this old philosopher with the grey whiskers. That is Euclid, professor of Geometry and Conic Sections. It is he who refuted the Sceptics. The Sceptics, your

Mightiness? They are philosophers who say that they know nothing at all, not even that they know nothing at all—and *even that* they do not know that they do not know. But Euclid has discovered certain Truths that all must admit. Observe him now, demonstrating upon the screen. I have attended his lectures, and I understand. He is now demonstrating that the two angles at the base of an isosceles triangle are equal. Listen to the cries of enthusiasm and delight with which the students hail his proof! Those cries from the farther room? Your Mightiness is right—*those* are not screams of enthusiasm and enjoyment, for that is the dissecting-room where students learn anatomy and all the wonders of the human frame. The city authorities allow us three criminals a week upon whom we may experiment for the advancement of science. The criminal whose screams you hear is a Nile boatman who stole three measures of meal from the public market. They are now operating upon his stomach, and I am told it is like to be a most entertaining and instructive lecture. Your Mightiness would prefer not to attend? It is as your Mightiness wishes; though I cannot but feel that much instruction and enjoyment will be missed.

These are the instruments of the Astronomers—armils, astrolabes, and the like; these are the halls for light reading and discussion of general topics. And these padded cells, marked 'Silence', are reserved for poets. Here also theologians sit in contemplation, for in the Museum six hundred different religions are represented. No, we have no trouble with them at all, except occasionally with the devil-worshippers.

And now we reach our original starting-point, and I have done. I humbly thank your Mightiness for your courtesy and attention, for the honour which you have done us by gracing the Museum with your kingly presence, and for the brace of panthers which you have so generously presented.

Notes

The following précis is quite straightforward. Start with Mr. Hunt's reasons for writing the letter, and then proceed with the events in the order in which they happened, leaving out all unessential talk.

This exercise will afford a good example of the following important rule:

RULE VII.—**Never put in any critical or explanatory remarks of your own.**

In this précis, for instance, one is tempted to point out that Mr. Hunt was *not* in a normal state, that on his own showing he was dreadfully depressed and lonely, and that this would affect the value of his evidence. But one must do nothing of the sort. One's business in this, as in every précis, is to write a concise summary of the story as it stands, and leave all criticism to the reader's common sense.

No. 13.—The Warning

Letter to the Secretary of the Psychical Research Society.

Sportsman's Hotel,
Alberta, Canada.

Dear Sir,

I should be glad if you would allow me to bring before the notice of the Society an amazing case of Forewarning which I myself have experienced. To my mind this extraordinary event carries with it its own evidence; for, had it not been for this premonition, I should not now be here to write the story. These are the facts, to which, if necessary, I am prepared to set my oath.

In the summer of the present year, 1910, I and my friend Colonel Symes arranged a grizzly-bear-shooting expedition in the Rocky Mountains. We wished to be entirely alone, and so we pushed off into the wilder country, eventually building our little hut just within the upper limits of the tree-line at a place marked on the enclosed map, a spot so remote that it has as yet no name.

Three weeks of excellent sport followed, and then calamity overtook us. While rounding a precipice path in Indian file we were met and attacked by a bear, and, before I could do anything to help, both the colonel and the bear had fallen over the cliff and were dashed onto the rocks below.

There was nothing to be done. Thirty seconds had sufficed to close our expedition in appalling disaster. I returned alone to the hut. For the rest of the day I wandered aimlessly round the clearing, trying in vain to make up my mind to return home to civilization. But I was numbed by the disaster, and after much barren thought I decided to put a double boarding onto the hut and stay where I was.

For the next five weeks I spent a solitary existence, living on what I shot and on the provisions which the Indian pack-horses had brought up when we first arrived. And then began the snow. It started little at first, and I cleared it away from the door of the hut. But soon the storms grew in violence, and before long all hunting was out of the question, and I spent my days in clearing a path from the hut door, and in reading over the camp stove.

On the fourth day of the blizzard the wind got up, and blew very hard with a most melancholy and dispiriting noise through the pine-trees above my hut. I felt wretchedly lonely; and, though I managed to pass the day in cooking meals and putting the finishing stitches to a heavy sleeping-suit of bear-skin, by the time darkness came on I was in the depths of depression.

At ten o'clock I turned in—that is, I rolled myself up on my bear-skin couch—and for half an hour I read in my copy of Shakespeare: showing that my mind was in a perfectly normal condition. At 10.30 I shut the stove, blew out the lantern, and went to sleep, the blizzard still raging with great violence outside.

It must have been about five hours later that I woke with a feeling of oppression and horror such as I had never before experienced. At first I was at a loss to understand the cause of my fright. I sat up, on one elbow, and shivered. Then I realized what it was—there was someone else in the room! Now the door was barred against wild animals; moreover I was full fifty miles from the nearest encampment. And the horror of this unseen presence made the hair crawl upon my scalp. I sat bolt upright and held my breath. It was then that a full perception of the Horror flooded in upon me like a wave—the Thing was lying on the couch by my side! It was pitch dark of course, and I could see nothing. I merely "sensed" this presence on the couch. With a leap I was across the room and lighting my lantern with trembling fingers. Then I returned to the couch.

I cannot attempt to express the horror of what I saw. My breathing stopped with a jerk and my heart stood still. For there was *myself* lying dead upon the couch, crushed across the body by some unseen and appalling weight!

I dropped the lamp, leapt to the door, and in a frenzy of terror staggered out into the storm. Twenty seconds passed—it can hardly have been more—when with a rending noise like an avalanche one of the great pine-trees fell clean across the centre of the hut, crushing it into matchwood!

As soon as it was day I pushed off for the lowlands (luckily my ski and gun were in the outhouse, and so escaped).

I have no evidence beyond the word of a gentleman to prove the truth of what I have narrated; I can only assure you of the absolute and literal truth of the premonition; though whether the apparition was an objective reality or a figment of my own imagination I must leave to the opinion of the Psychical Research Society.

Believe me, Sir,

Yours very truly,

NIMROD HUNT.

Notes

In the following précis do not proceed by question and answer. Arrange the subjects in definite groups as you think best.

The main point to remember is that you *must not criticize* this wonderful medley of nonsense. All you have to do is to give a concise idea of the kind of pseudo-science that boys had to learn by heart a hundred and fifty years ago. (The original is largely taken from old school-books.) You must not use a single phrase such as 'this absurd idea'. Your *title* should imply that such stuff is very much out-of-date.

No. 14.—Science as taught in our Great-grandfathers' School-days

Preceptor. What is Science?

Child. Science is the investigation and proper appreciation of the phenomena of the Universe in which it has pleased the Creator to place us. This investigation is applied to the Elements and to the Immutable Laws which govern them.

Preceptor. How many Elements are there?

Child. Four: Fire, Water, Earth, and Air—the Igneous element, the Aqueous element, the Earthy, and the Aerial elements.

Preceptor. What is Fire?

Child. Fire, or the Igneous element, is the element of destruction. It consists of flame, which devours materials, and imparts a comfortable warmth to man and beast. The sun is the primary source of heat; the interior of the Earth consists of Fire; combustion can be produced artificially by man; and the Lightning is its most terrific manifestation.

Preceptor. What is Lightning?

Child. Lightning is a large bright flame darting through the air to a considerable distance, of momentary duration, and usually accompanied by thunder.

Preceptor. What is Thunder?

Child. Thunder is a loud rattling noise accompanied by Lightning, caused by the sudden clashing or rushing together of several clouds which are filled with sulphurous and nitrous exhalations. Its reverberations fill the hearer with awe, and turn the mind to thoughts of piety and submission.

Preceptor. What is the Earthy element?

Child. The Earthy element is the solid ground upon which we live. It is divided into mountains, hills, valleys, and plains, in a variety pleasing to the eye, and adapted to all sorts and conditions of men.

Preceptor. Of what is the Earthy element composed?

Child. The Earth is composed of rocks, sand, metals, and mud, in which are also to be found the more precious stones, such as the diamond, the jacynth, the topaz, and the chrysoprasus.

Preceptor. When was the Earth created?

Child. The Earth was created by the Divine Will in the year 4004 B.C., the sun, moon, and stars, being created shortly afterwards for the use and benefit of man.

Preceptor. How were the Mountains formed?

Child. For the first few thousand years it would seem that the Earth was subjected to occasional violent catastrophes, both by fire and water. In these catastrophes great mountain chains were sometimes flung up; at other times the waters swept over the tops of the hills, and the shells of sea creatures may be found there to this day.

Preceptor. Have these catastrophes ceased?

Child. They have become less violent in their nature, though the recent Earthquake and Wave at Lisbon and the Eruption of Mount Hecla in Iceland attest their continued activity.

Preceptor. What is the Aerial Element?

Child. It is that elastic fluid with which the Earth is surrounded. It is generally called Air. It partakes of all the motions of the earth.

Preceptor. What is the cause of the Wind?

Child. The cause of the Wind has never been ascertained.

Preceptor. Then are the Winds of no benefit to us?

Child. Yes, the benefits arising from them are innumerable: they dry the damp, they chase vile humours, they bring us the rain in due season, and waft our ships from every corner of the Earth.

Preceptor. What is the Aqueous element?

Child. The Aqueous element is generally called Water. It is the fluid which covers half the surface of the Globe, and it is divided into seas and oceans. It is also manifested in rivers, streams, springs, rain, and mist.

Preceptor. Why is the sea salt?

Child. The saltness of the sea is due to certain saline properties in water when brought together in very large quantities.

Preceptor. Do we derive any advantage from the study of Science and Natural Philosophy?

Child. Yes; for without a competent knowledge of Natural Philosophy we cannot form a true conception of the Purpose of Creation; nor can we adapt our daily lives in accordance with the Law by which all things work together for the benefit and improvement of Mankind.

Notes

It is very important to be able to make a précis of a number of letters or telegrams.

RULE VIII.—**In making a précis of a number of letters DO NOT PROCEED LETTER BY LETTER. Get the gist of the whole story; then pick out the important points and arrange them in the order in which the events happened. Several letters or telegrams may be combined in one paragraph, if they are on the same topic, but the topics must be kept separate.**

RULE IX.—**Never omit the principal DATES AND TIMES.**

No. 15—The Hut-Tax

Correspondence between the Administrator of British Bongoland, the Commissioner of the M'Gobi District, and the Colonial Secretary.

1. To Mr. Commissioner Philips:—

From GOVERNMENT HOUSE, BONGOLAND.
June 1.

There has been a serious falling off in the income from your district, for which it is difficult to account. You will therefore kindly increase the Hut-tax to the extent of 2 pounds of rubber and 10 brass rods per hut. Kindly acquaint me when this has been done.

O. F. Administrator.

2. To the Administrator:—

From COMMISSIONER'S HUT, M'GOBI DISTRICT.
June 14.

SIR,

I have the honour to report that the utmost possible has been done in the matter of collecting taxes. The people have suffered great hardship this year owing to sleeping-sickness, and though the disease has been stamped out, labour has been scarce, and I do not feel justified in advising H.M. Government to increase the tax.

I have the honour to be,

Your Obedient Servant,

H. PHILIPS.

3. To Mr. Commissioner Philips:—

From GOVERNMENT HOUSE.
July 1.

You are not expected to advise H.M. Government. Kindly collect the tax as I order, and report to me later.

O. F. Administrator.

4. To the Administrator:—

From COMMISSIONER'S HUT, M'GOBI DISTRICT.
July 11.

SIR,

I have the honour to inform you, from evidence obtained on the spot, that any attempt to levy an extra tax will be attended with serious consequences—disorder and probable loss of life. I therefore cannot hold myself responsible for the lives of missionaries and other white men in the district in case the tax is levied.

I have the honour to be,

Your Obedient Servant,

H. PHILIPS.

5. To Mr. Commissioner Philips:—

From GOVERNMENT HOUSE.
July 20.

You may take what steps you like with regard to missionaries; but the tax must be collected.

O. F. Administrator.

(For Précis. Paper 2.)

6. (By telegram.)

To the Administrator, British Bongoland:—

From COLONIAL OFFICE, WHITEHALL.
July 30.

SIR,

Roman Catholic and Protestant missionaries in M'Gobi district report having been removed to coast by order of Mr. Commissioner Philips. Danger apprehended from levy of extra Hut-tax. H.M. Government is very averse to the imposition of harsh taxes, and I must therefore ask you to delay collection and furnish information without delay.

HEDLEY: Assist. Sec.

7. (By telegram.)

To the Colonial Office:—

From BRITISH BONGOLAND.
Aug. 1.

SIR,

I am not accustomed to having my actions criticized. You may leave this matter entirely in my hands.

I have the honour to be,

Your Obedient Servant,

OBADIAH FITZBLANK,
Administrator.

8. (By telegram.)

To Sir Obadiah FitzBlank:—

From COLONIAL OFFICE, WHITEHALL.
Aug. 2, 1 p.m.

You will inform Mr. Commissioner Philips that H.M. Government are of opinion, in agreement with him, that the new tax should not be imposed. You will also resign your office immediately and return by the boat that leaves to-morrow night. Your successor has already left.

JOSEPH CHAMBERLAIN.

Notes

Remember Rule VIII and Rule IX.

Also, it is often convenient to use a *general* term instead of names: such as 'The Naval Authorities' or 'The British Government'.

No. 16.—The Mandarin

Correspondence concerning the bastinadoing of a British subject in the village of Ching-Wang, 30 miles from Shang-Hai.

1. To the British Consul at Shang-Hai:—

From CHING-WANG.
April 2.

SIR,

I write to say as how I have been bastinadoed on both feet. My feet is swole something cruel. This was done by the Mandarin Lu-Chu. He says as how I stole his cherries, which I never done it. Please investigate. I am a British subjick, which my mother was a Chinee.

Yours truly,

FU-LING THOMPSON.

2. To His Complacency the Mandarin Lu-Chu:—

From CONSUL'S HOUSE, SHANG-HAI.
April 8.

Having been informed by the half-caste Fu-Ling Thompson, a British subject, that corporal punishment had been unjustly inflicted upon him by your orders, I sent my agent to investigate the matter. He informs me that Thompson speaks the truth, and that you yourself are perfectly aware of the man's innocence. I therefore suggest that, to avoid complications with H.M. Government, you compensate Mr. Thompson to the extent of £50 or 100,000 sens.

H. CASLON, British Consul.

3. (Translation.)

To the British Consul:—

From CHING-WANG.

Almighty Consul whose face shines like the moon. I cannot give Mr. Thompson 100,000 sens, for I am a poor man. Moreover, the cherries were stolen. It was right and fitting that someone should be bastinadoed.

LU-CHU.

4. To Lieut.-Commander Hanlon of H.M.S. *Laverock*:—

(Per picket boat.)

From CONSUL'S HOUSE, SHANG-HAI.
April 12.

DEAR HANLON,

The Mandarin of Ching-Wang has been up to his old tricks again—bastinadoing a British subject. I have ordered him to pay the man £50 and he refuses. I suggest that you make a demonstration. (Correspondence enclosed.)

Yours,

H. CASLON.

5. (By Wireless.)

To Admiral Groves, China Station:—

April 12.

Another case of unjustified bastinadoing. Mandarin refuses compensation. What steps may I take?

HANLON,
Lieut.-Commander.

6. (By Wireless from H.M.S. *Thunderer*):—

Leave entirely in your hands. Use great firmness but avoid complications.

GROVES,
Admiral.

7. From H.M.S. *Laverock* (by letter):—

April 13.

To his Complacency the Mandarin Lu-Chu.

In the matter of the bastinadoing of Mr. Thompson, a British subject, the case as you know has been investigated, and I am authorized to demand the immediate payment of 100,000 sens. Unless this demand is complied with before 4 o'clock, I shall be reluctantly compelled to blow your house to pieces.

HANLON,
Lieut.-Commander.

8. To Lieut.-Commander Hanlon (translation):—

Most superb Lieutenant-Commander, whose guns roar like many devils. I cannot pay Mister Thompson 100,000 sens, for I am a poor man. Moreover, I did but beat him upon the soles of his feet.

LU-CHU.

9. To the British Consul at Shang-Hai:—

From H.M.S. *Laverock*.
April 14.

DEAR CASLON,

Lu-Chu flatly refused to pay; so, with the Admiral's leave, I took the law into my own hands. At ten past four I stood right into the harbour and fired a large wad of cotton-waste into his cherry-trees. The old fellow was frightened out of his life, and sent the money within five minutes.

Yours,

J. Hanlon.

Notes

Rule X.—**ALWAYS KEEP A PROPER BALANCE. That is to say, it often happens that in the original too much space is given to picturesque details, and too little to the more important facts. In your précis this must be put right.**

This is obviously the case in the following Life of Isaac Newton.

No. 17—Isaac Newton

Newton was born in 1643, and was the smallest baby in the world. He went to school when very young, but does not appear to have done any work till one day the top-boy kicked him violently in the stomach for daring to get his sums right. Then Newton began to work, not with any idea of becoming the greatest of mathematicians, but simply because he resented being kicked in the stomach, and determined to get the better of his tormentor. His spare time was spent in making ingenious little contrivances, water-clocks, paper lamps attached to kites with which to frighten the villagers, a 'wind-mill' turned by a pet mouse with a string tied to its tail. When he left school he was tried on the farm, but it was no use. Newton was always behind a hedge inventing some new automatic toy, while the pigs wallowed in clover, and the cows trampled down the corn. So he went to Trinity College, Cambridge, and there his serious studies began.

His first discoveries were on the subject of light, about which very little was then known. On darkening his room and allowing a circular beam of sunlight to pass through a hole in the shutter, and thence through a triangular glass prism, he found that an oblong patch of light was cast on the screen five times as long as the hole in the shutter. Moreover, it was no longer white, but made up of all the colours of the rainbow—violet, indigo, blue, green, yellow, orange, red—always ranged in the same order. He soon came to the conclusion that white is not a separate colour, but is made up of all the colours of the 'spectrum'.

He next invented the reflecting telescope, forerunner of all the vast instruments by means of which the wonders of the sky have been investigated.

He then turned his great mind to the problem of finding out what light really is, and, though his theory has been given up for a better, it was the best that had been suggested up to that time. He also found out that light travels at the rate of nearly 200,000 miles a second.

Meanwhile the Plague broke out at Cambridge, making it necessary for him to retire into the country. It was in the garden of his country house that the fall of an apple is supposed to have suggested to Newton the theory of gravitation.

Scientists had for a long time been familiar with the fact that the earth is a colossal magnet, drawing everything upon its surface in the direction of its centre; but it was Newton who conceived the idea—and whether it was the falling apple that suggested it or no is unimportant—that the influence extended as far as the moon, and, if this could be established, to the stars throughout space. Was it not possible that the moon, trying to shoot off at a tangent, was continually pulled back by the earth, and so kept 'falling' round it? Newton tried experiments, applying laws already discovered, and found that the theory would not work. Undiscouraged he put the whole problem aside till more facts should have been discovered. It was not till 1682 that more accurate measurements of the earth gave Newton fresh data to go upon. Again he applied his theory, and this time he began to see that his problem was 'coming out'—that the moon would fall just the right distance, 15 feet per minute. As he neared the end of his calculations he became so agitated that he could not go on: a friend had to finish it for him. And it was right. He had established the fact that not only is the moon subject to the law of gravitation, but that the whole universe is slung together in one stupendous system.

It is this grand discovery, and the wonderful invention of the calculus, that establish Newton's claim to immortal honour. As says the inscription in Westminster Abbey: "The vigour of his mind was almost supernatural".

Notes

In this précis the story should be condensed, and told as a continuous narrative, and not in scraps and jottings as in a log.

For the purpose of verifying positions, &c.—especially as the battle was fought at night—it is important to mention *names* of all ships.

It is also necessary to give the *times* of the chief events; but one can avoid monotony and scrappiness by using phrases such as "Ten minutes later...."

No. 18.—The Battle of the Nile

From the log of the *Swiftsure* (unofficial):—

At 6.0 p.m. received order from Flag-ship to furl and wet all unused sails; and to sling a cross-bar to the mizzen peak with four ship's lanterns; also to sling a ship's lantern over each gun-port, as the fight would be in the dark, and friend must be distinguished from foe. Superintended the sanding of decks, and final arrangements. 6.30, the fight began. French land batteries opened on the *Goliath*, which ship, followed by the *Theseus* and others, rounded the tip of the French line and dropped anchor on the shoal side. By 7.0 it was dark, the battle raging furiously apparently on both sides of the enemy van. At 7.15 received message from Captain Troubridge of the *Culloden* that he was on the sands. Put helm over and kept away to eastwards. 7.30, sailed down the battle line looking for an enemy's ship to lie alongside. Sighted a vessel in movement. Order given to stand to the guns, for she showed no lights. Hailed ship, and received answer: "This is the *Bellerophon* going out of action disabled". Passed close under stern of *Bellerophon*. She had apparently lost both main and foremasts, and much wreckage lay over her sides. As far as could be distinguished in the darkness she appeared to be just under control, carrying on under mizzen and sprit sail. 7.40, order given to take *Bellerophon's* place in fight. At 8.3 let go one small bower anchor in seven fathoms of water. At 8.5 commenced firing at a two-decked ship called the *Franklin* on the starboard quarter, and a three-decked ship called *L'Orient* on starboard bow. Apparently *L'Orient* was some 200 yards from our ship. She was using all three tiers of guns, but some had been put out of action by the *Bellerophon*. At 8.30 the *Alexander* also closed on *L'Orient* [added later: she was French Flag-ship] and the fight became very furious. At 9.3 *L'Orient* caught fire. Order given to isolate *L'Orient's* poop with cannon and musket-fire, to prevent the flames being put out. (In the glare much loose gear, such as paint-pots could be seen scattered on the poop.) At a quarter to 10 *L'Orient* blew up. Most of the wreckage fell into the sea; some on to the deck of the *Swiftsure* but without inflicting casualties. Hove in cable. Lowered two boats, in charge of midshipmen. Picked up nine men and one lieutenant who escaped out of *L'Orient*. Saw the *Alexander's* bowsprit and her main-topgallant sail to be on fire. At 10.20 ceased firing. Sent Lieutenant Cowen to take possession of the enemy's ship, the *Franklin*, that lay on our quarter, who hailed us that she had struck, with her main mizzen-masts gone. At 10.35 he returned, finding that she was taken possession of by an officer from the *Defence*. At 10.50 saw the *Alexander* and another ship, which proved to be the *Majestic*, engaging the enemy's ships to the left of us at about a mile. Bore down to their assistance. For the next four hours engaged enemy's ships to the rear of their line. Enemy's fire became wild and inflicted little damage. At 3 a.m. order was given to cease fire. Guns' crews much exhausted, many of the men lying on the gun decks, their arms swollen from continuous work at the out-hauls. Order given for the distribution of rum and coffee. At 5.30 saw that six of the enemy's ships at our end of the line had struck their colours. Our carpenters employed stopping the shot-holes. People employed knotting and splicing the rigging. At 6 the *Majestic* fired her minute guns on interring her captain, who was killed in the action.